DISCARD

INNOVATORS

Stephanie Kwolek

Creator of Kevlar

Other titles in the Innovators series include:

Tim Burton: Filmmaker
Jonathan Ive: Designer of the iPod
Ken Kutaragi: PlayStation Developer
John Lasseter: Pixar Animator
Shigeru Miyamoto: Nintendo Game Designer
Pierre M. Omidyar: Creator of eBay
Larry Page and Sergey Brin: The Google Guys
Burt Rutan: Aircraft Designer
Shel Silverstein: Poet
Frederick W. Smith: Founder of FedEx

INNOVATORS

Stephanie Kwolek

Creator of Kevlar

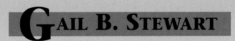
GAIL B. STEWART

KIDHAVEN PRESS
A part of Gale, Cengage Learning

GALE
CENGAGE Learning™

Detroit • New York • San Francisco • New Haven, Conn • Waterville, Maine • London

GALE
CENGAGE Learning·

LIBRARY OF CONGRESS CATALOGING-IN-PUBLICATION DATA

Stewart, Gail B. (Gail Barbara), 1949–
    Stephanie Kwolek : creator of Kevlar / by Gail B. Stewart.
      p. cm. — (Innovators)
    Includes bibliographical references and index.
    ISBN-13: 978-0-7377-4040-0 (hardcover)
    1. Kwolek, Stephanie, 1923—Juvenile literature. 2. Industrial chemists—United States—Biography—Juvenile literature. 3. Inventors—United States—Biography—Juvenile literature. 4. Ballistic fabrics—Juvenile literature. 5. Polyphenyleneterephthalamide—Juvenile literature. I. Title.
    TS1440.K96S74 2008
    660.092—dc22
    [B]
                                                                            2008009190

KidHaven Press
27500 Drake Rd.
Farmington Hills, MI 48331

ISBN-13: 978-0-7377-4040-0
ISBN-10: 0-7377-4040-X

Printed in the United States of America
1 2 3 4 5 6 7 12 11 10 09 08

CONTENTS

Introduction 6
   "Not in a Million Years"

Chapter One 9
   A Childhood in Pennsylvania

Chapter Two 16
   Choosing Research

Chapter Three 23
   "I Thought It Could Be a Mistake
      Somehow"

Chapter Four 31
   Kevlar and Beyond

Notes 39
Glossary 41
For Further Exploration 42
Index 44
Picture Credits 47
About the Author 48

"Not in a Million Years"

On October 8, 2005, Atlanta police officer Corey Grogan was in trouble. He and a team of other officers had located a criminal who was wanted for several violent crimes. As they approached the man's house to arrest him, shots rang out. The man shot one of Grogan's fellow officers. As Grogan rushed to reach the wounded officer and pull him out of the line of fire, the suspect aimed his gun at Grogan's chest and pulled the trigger twice.

Grogan felt the first shot slam against his chest. The second shot knocked him down. Although the bullets had found their mark, he was not seriously hurt. Like many police officers, Grogan was wearing a special vest underneath his uniform's shirt. It was made of a material that bullets could not completely penetrate.

Grogan says he owes his life to the vest, because without it, doctors told him he would have died. "I'm thankful for that vest," he says with emotion. "It's allowed me to be here today, to do the job that I love."[1]

Two police officers conduct an investigation while wearing bulletproof vests. Many officers' lives have been saved thanks to the vests.

"You Never Know Where a Discovery Will Lead"

The protective material in the clothing worn by Grogan and other police officers is made of a **fiber** called Kevlar. The fiber is five times stronger than steel. It can stop bullets, as Grogan and thousands of other police officers and soldiers know first-hand. But it was not invented to stop bullets. In fact, the invention of Kevlar was a surprise—an unexpected discovery.

Stephanie Kwolek, the woman who invented Kevlar, was a research scientist for DuPont, a chemical company. She says that many times a scientist makes a discovery without knowing

Unlike today, when Stephanie Kwolek began her career in 1946 it was rare to find female scientists in laboratories.

how important it might later become. That, she says, is what makes science so exciting. "Not in a million years did I expect that this fiber would end up saving thousands of lives," she says. "You never know where a discovery will lead."[2]

People can be as unpredictable as discoveries. This is true of Kwolek as well. When Kwolek began her career in 1946, women were rare in science laboratories. Although she became a pioneer for women scientists, she did not plan to be. "I just wanted to be a scientist," she explains. "I wasn't thinking of being a woman scientist. I just loved the work. I loved making discoveries and learning things as I went along."[3]

The story of Stephanie Kwolek is one of hard work and determination. It is also proof that the most amazing things can happen when one least expects them.

CHAPTER 1

A Childhood in Pennsylvania

Kwolek did not know she would become a scientist when she was young. But early in life, she was curious about the world around her. She was confident and eager to learn. Her mother and father encouraged those qualities from the time their daughter was very young.

A Daughter of Immigrants

Kwolek was born on July 23, 1923, in New Kensington, Pennsylvania. Her parents, John and Nellie, were Polish immigrants who came to the United States while in their teens. Kwolek says that her mother and a friend, a girl from the same village in Poland, made the long journey alone just before World War I. They traveled from Poland to Hamburg, Germany, to board the boat that would take them to America.

"I was amazed how adventurous my mother was," says Kwolek. "I have a picture of them in my house now, the two young friends in Hamburg. They bought new clothes for the

Kwolek's parents were Polish immigrants, like the ones pictured here, who came to the United States while just teenagers.

journey, and they look quite stylish—high-button shoes and hats with big brims. They were so brave, and were having so much fun. What an adventure they must have had!"[4]

Nellie met John Kwolek in New Kensington. Both took rooms at the same place after they arrived from Poland. "Lots of single people from overseas did that—took rooms in boarding-houses," says Kwolek. "It was cheaper than finding a house or apartment. Anyway, it was not long before they met, fell in love and married."[5] John got a job at a nearby factory, and Nellie stayed at home to raise Stephanie and her brother, Stanley, two years younger.

"They Were Both Smart"

Kwolek remembers that her parents were very determined that their children get as much education as possible in their new country. "I'm not sure how educated my mother was," she says. "But she read a lot. And she and my father picked up English very quickly—they were very good English speakers. They were both smart. They did speak Polish at home, and I learned some, too."[6]

One of the ways her mother helped in Kwolek's education was teaching her to sew. It was the time of the Great Depression, and many people were very poor. "It was important to know how to do a lot of things for yourself back then," Kwolek says. "She made a lot of my clothes. She was really very good, too— good enough to have been a professional seamstress, if she'd wanted. That was a skill she wanted me to have as well."[7]

Kwolek's father instilled in her an interest in science. The two of them spent a lot of time exploring the woods and creeks near their home. He taught her about the animals and plants that lived there. The two collected flowers, seeds, and leaves, so she could study them at home. She saved them by pressing them in a notebook. Stephanie and her father also brought fruit home. "We'd pick huckleberries and take them home," says Kwolek. "My mother would bake pies."[8]

"A Horrible, Horrible Thing"

That was a very happy time in her life. Young Stephanie enjoyed playing with other children on the outskirts of town. "I was never shy," she laughs. "I was an active child, playing kick the can and other games children played back then. We had lots of room to roam, and that made it an especially fun time of my life."[9]

But the carefree time of being young ended for Stephanie at age ten. Her father, still a young man at age forty, suffered a heart attack. He had surgery, but soon it was clear that he would not survive. Even more than seventy years later, she shudders when she thinks of that time.

"To this day, I have a very vivid memory of [my brother] Stanley and I being taken to the hospital. We were to say a last good-bye to our father," she says. "He was gasping for breath. It was so hard to see him that way. It was a horrible, horrible thing."[10]

Planning for the Future

After her husband's death, Nellie Kwolek had to go to work to provide for her two children. The Aluminum Company of America (Alcoa) plant was located nearby, and she got a job there. "We weren't able to do things like sewing very often together after that," says Kwolek. "My mother worked very hard, and there just wasn't as much time for doing those things when my father died."[11]

Stephanie had always been a good student, and she continued to work hard. She loved to read, and she tried her hand at

Like the family pictured here, Kwolek and her family lived during the Great Depression and were very poor.

writing poetry. As she entered high school, she thought about what she would do with her life. One thing she was sure of—she did not want to become a wife and mother right away, like so many girls of that time. "It was very common, getting married right after high school," she says. "But I wanted to go to

A man works at the Alcoa plant where Kwolek's mother Nellie got a job after her husband's death.

college. I enjoyed going to dances and having fun. But I was not ready for a serious boyfriend."[12]

Instead, she thought about a number of careers. Her sewing had sparked an interest in being a clothing designer. She loved the idea of creating something new. But her mother laughingly warned her that she might starve in that job, because Stephanie was such a **perfectionist**. It took her a long time to finish a project, and even then, she was rarely happy with it. Another dream came from her nature walks with her father. She thought about being a scientist of some sort—perhaps a doctor. With that goal in mind, she spent more time studying and preparing for college. Whatever she did with her life, she vowed that she would be good at it.

CHAPTER 2

Choosing Research

In 1942, after graduating from high school, Kwolek enrolled in a women's college in Pittsburgh called Margaret Morrison Carnegie College. It was part of a larger all-men's university, known today as Carnegie Mellon University. By this time, she was certain that she wanted to be a scientist—probably a medical doctor.

To achieve her goal, she knew she must study hard. There were few women doctors in those days. If the decision to go to college was unusual for a young woman, studying science was quite rare. But Kwolek did not worry about it. "I was pretty sure of myself," she says, looking back. "I didn't think about myself as a woman studying science. I thought of myself as a college student studying science. I knew I could do it."[13]

An Unusual Time

Kwolek has **bittersweet** memories of college. She loved the challenge of her studies. When her college did not offer a science

A building on the campus of Carnegie Mellon University in Pittsburgh, Pennsylvania. Kwolek attended a women's college called Margaret Morrison Carnegie College, which was part of Carnegie Mellon.

class she needed, she was able to take the class at the nearby men's university. She found her interests expanding. For example, she realized that she not only had a talent for biology (the study of living things), but she was fascinated by **chemistry** as well.

She also enjoyed the friendship of a wide circle of friends. She and her friends played a lot of bridge—a popular card game among college students in the 1940s. She remembers the journeys back and forth between Pittsburgh and New Kensington on the train during school vacations with masses of college students. "It seemed as if the whole train was playing cards,"[14] she says.

But while many parts of college life were fun, there was a shadow over that time. It was the height of World War II. After the bombing of Pearl Harbor on December 7, 1941, the United States had entered the war, too. By 1942, when Kwolek began college, young Americans (mostly men) were heading off to war. Many of those were college students. Kwolek says that seeing them leave remains a very sad memory for her.

"All the young men suddenly were gone," she says. "Brothers, boyfriends, friends—it was awful. They were put on boxcars on trains and sent off down south to the basic camps someplace. Believe me, it was very, very painful to watch. So many boys, so young. We would go down to the railroad station and watch as they were put in the cars. We would wave and cry as they left—a terrible time."[15]

An Introduction to Research

With so many young men leaving for the war, more positions opened for women. During the summers Kwolek got a job at the University of Pittsburgh Medical School. It was a research position, one that would have usually gone to a young male graduate student. It was thrilling for her to be able to do research, even though she was still an undergraduate.

Her job was to do research on a chemical found in rat's blood. "Don't ask me what I was looking for—I don't remember," says Kwolek, and adds, "I was glad I didn't have to kill the rats, since I would not have been able to do that. But it was very exciting to be doing real research on my own."[16]

The highest point of that research occurred later that summer. The University of Pittsburgh was trying to hire a professor from Switzerland. The university staff invited him to visit, hoping to impress him so that he would join their faculty. They organized an event where several of the people in the medical school shared the research they were doing.

Kwolek, then only nineteen years old, was stunned when they invited her to talk, too. Although she was terrified, she was also excited and proud that the faculty had confidence in her. She had always dreamed of being a doctor. And while that was still her goal, she now realized how satisfying research could be.

Putting a Dream on Hold

When Kwolek graduated from college in 1946, she had to change her plans. Medical school was very expensive. She had to get a job and make some money so she could afford to attend. Her work in the university research lab had been rewarding, so she looked for another job doing research.

She interviewed at several companies. The Gulf Oil Company made her an offer, but she was more intrigued by a new company called DuPont. DuPont was a chemical company that was experimenting with **synthetic** fabrics. These materials were created in a laboratory, unlike natural fabrics like wool or cotton.

Although Kwolek was offered a job at the Gulf Oil Company, she was more interested in the work that DuPont was doing and was excited when they made her a job offer.

Eight years before, researchers at DuPont had invented **nylon**, a material soft enough to be used for clothing, but strong enough to be made into rope.

Kwolek went to DuPont for a job interview. The interviewer was impressed by her research work. He told her that he would consider her for the job. "He told me he'd let me know in two weeks," she remembers. "But I did something that I guess was pretty bold—especially for a woman in those days. I told him that I had other offers. I said I wanted to find out sooner, so I could let those companies know. I was surprised when he called in his secretary. He dictated a job offer for me right there."[17]

Working with Polymers

The new job was fascinating. The researchers at DuPont were trying to come up with new synthetic fabrics. This involved working with **polymers**, long chains made up of thousands— sometimes hundreds of thousands—of **molecules**. By combining and arranging molecules in new ways, researchers were

A computer illustration of a polymer's molecular structure. When Kwolek began working at DuPont she had no idea that she herself would discover a new polymer.

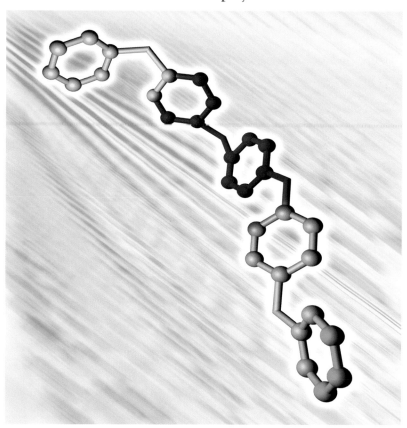

In 1964 DuPont put Kwolek to work trying to develop a fiber for a tire that would not melt, break, or rip when exposed to heat.

A Scientist's Method

Research scientists always follow set routines in the laboratory. Kwolek's first step was to combine various substances to make a polymer. Next, she would melt the polymer into a liquid.

Once it was in liquid form, the polymer was put into a special machine called a **spinneret**. The spinneret operates like a

hypodermic needle used in a doctor's office to give a shot. In a hypodermic needle the medicine is put into a glass capsule containing a little plunger. When the doctor pushes down on the plunger, the medicine flows through a tiny hole in the needle into the patient's arm.

In the same way, a spinneret operator puts the liquid polymer into a capsule. By forcing a plunger down (called "spinning"), the liquid comes out not one hole, but 1,000 tiny holes in what looks like the nozzle of a garden hose. Each of the holes is no more than .001 inch (.0254 mm) in diameter.

The 1,000 streams of polymers emerge into very cold water, which makes them solid again. At this point, they are fibers. These fibers are taken to another part of the lab, where they are tested. Researchers carefully watch them under different conditions. They weigh them and evaluate how strong they are. They also perform tests to see whether the fibers stretch easily and whether they are flexible.

Not Like Molasses

One day in 1965, Kwolek was working with a polymer that would not melt. Heating it did not work. She searched for a special substance, called a **solvent,** that could melt the polymer. Then she noticed something strange. In fact, she recalls, the polymer solution looked like nothing she had ever seen in the lab.

"Ordinarily a polymer solution sort of reminds you of molasses [syrup], although it may not be as thick. And it's generally transparent [clear]. This polymer solution poured almost like water, and it was cloudy."[19]

When she stirred it, the solution was even stranger. It separated into a light yellow layer, which was clear, and a cloudy layer. Kwolek says it would have been easy just to write off that solution and to start over. But she didn't. In fact, she remembers being intrigued by the solution's odd appearance, although she admits it looked more like a mistake than anything useful. "I think someone who wasn't thinking very much, or who just wasn't aware or took less interest in it," she says, "would have thrown it out."[20]

"This Will Never Spin"

Kwolek decided to take the strange yellowish solution to the next step—the spinneret. But the man who worked the machine took

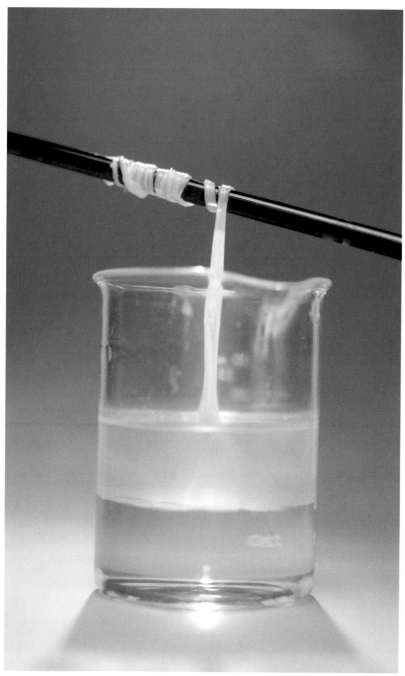

A polymer solution is melted in order to make nylon. This solution is much thicker than the polymer solution used to make Kevlar.

one look at the cloudy liquid and shook his head. "He said to me, 'This will never spin, it flows like water. And, furthermore, it has particles in it that will plug up the holes of the spinneret.'"[21]

Kwolek says that she kept asking him, pestering him to try it. She told him she did not believe there were particles in the solution. She said that the polymer solution could be something valuable. It took days, but he eventually gave in and agreed to test it. "I think either I wore him down," she says, "or else he felt sorry for me."[22]

As Kwolek hoped, the solution did no damage to the spinneret machine. But what emerged was very unusual. Usually the polymer fibers that emerged from the 1,000 tiny holes of the machine were the consistency of cooked spaghetti—very flexible. But these fibers were very stiff, like matchsticks. Still puzzled, she took the fibers to the next step, the physical testing lab.

"I Wouldn't Tell Anyone at First"

The numbers from the testing were amazing. They showed that the fibers were nine times stiffer than any fiber that she had ever made in the lab. The strength was due to microscopic crystals. The crystals had formed because of the shape and structure of the molecules in the polymer that she had created. These crystals gave the solution its cloudy look.

Instead of being excited about her discovery, Kwolek did not say anything. "I wouldn't tell anyone at first," she says. "I thought it could be a mistake somehow. I really didn't want to be embarrassed by announcing something that turned out to be nothing more than a mistake, you know."[23]

She had a feeling that it was not a mistake, however. She tried to cut the fibers with scissors, but with no luck. They were stronger and more lightweight than anything she had ever seen. But just to be sure, she sent down sample after sample to the lab. Each time, the numbers came back the same. "I knew it was right, then," she says. "I felt it was safe to tell my coworkers and management. And it was so thrilling, really a very special feeling."[24]

Kwolek discovered that Kevlar fibers, like the ones shown here, were stronger and more lightweight than any other material known to scientists.

Kwolek's announcement caused a lot of excitement in the DuPont lab. Though no one knew then how the strange new fibers would be used, it seemed that a new chapter was beginning for synthetic fibers. And it all began with what seemed like a mistake. "A lot of luck," Kwolek agrees. "You just never know when things just work out. And what a wonderful feeling it is when something like this happens."[25]

CHAPTER 4

Kevlar and Beyond

Her discovery in the laboratory was just the beginning. "There was no time for celebrating," Kwolek says. "We had to figure out how to use the fiber—how to sell it."[26] The original goal of her research had been to make lighter tires. However, the tire industry was not interested. They claimed the new fiber would be too expensive.

"A Real Team Effort"

Even so, everyone at DuPont believed the fiber had great potential, though no one was sure yet how it would be used. The company assembled teams of people to handle particular jobs. One team worked on developing the fiber into commercial products (or goods that could be sold for money). Another worked on submitting patents—official documents stating that DuPont had invented the polymer fiber.

One team was in charge of naming the fiber. After a lot of ideas were looked at, Kevlar was the name chosen. "It doesn't

Spools of Kevlar thread, which testing proved were five times stronger than steel.

mean anything," says Kwolek. "But it has a hard, tough sound to it—I think because of the *k* sound. And because the fiber is tough and durable, the name should reflect that. You know, other DuPont fibers were softer sounding, like nylon and Orlon®. Those letters sound soft, and that's because the fibers were made for soft clothing. But this one had to be different."[27]

Testing proved that Kevlar was five times stronger than steel, although it was very light. That was impressive, but caused other problems for the company. The machines used to manufacture nylon and other soft fabrics would not work for Kevlar. New machines and cutting tools had to be created to work with the new fiber. Kwolek says that although she discovered the fiber, a great amount of work was done afterwards by others at the company. "It was a real team effort,"[28] she says.

Bulletproof

It took almost ten years for the first products using Kevlar to appear on the market. Since its invention, Kevlar has been used in more than two hundred products. Because it is strong and light, it is used to make canoes, skis, racing helmets, cables for securing bridges, and airplane parts. Because it resists heat, it is used to make everything from oven mitts to firefighters' suits and the outer shells of spaceships.

All of its uses have proved to be valuable. None, however, has been as important as the Kevlar bulletproof vest, a garment worn by police and other law enforcement officers. The idea of bulletproof clothing was not new. World War II bomber pilots sometimes stuffed heavy metal plates in their shirts to try to protect themselves from gunners on enemy airplanes. Instead of blocking bullets, the Kevlar fibers in the vest actually disperse,

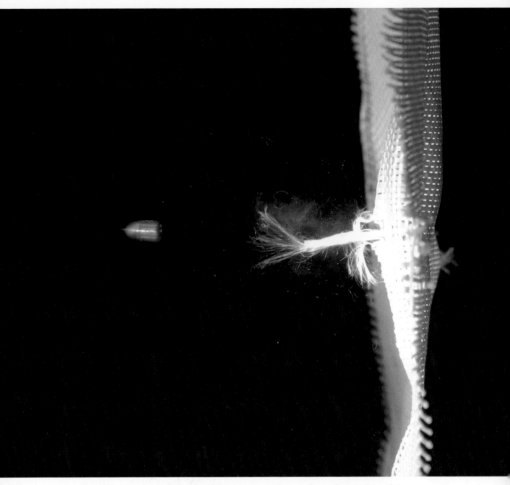

As a bullet passes through material made of Kevlar fiber, its speed and impact are dispersed.

or spread out, the force of a bullet's impact. That way, a bullet does not penetrate the skin, because its speed and impact is scattered in different directions.

Since 1975, when the Kevlar vest was first made, it has saved the lives of more than 3,000 people. In Iraq and Afghanistan, U.S. soldiers wear Kevlar reinforced with special plates to protect them from assault rifles and other powerful weapons of war. David Nelson, a deputy manager in charge of uniforms and equipment for the army, calls Kevlar "one of the most significant pieces of military equipment ever invented."[29]

A Forty-Year Career

Kwolek's work did not stop with the invention of Kevlar. She worked for another twenty years at DuPont, continuing her research on high-powered fibers like Kevlar. Because of her, DuPont has seventeen more patents on new fibers and the processes to make them.

She has received more than thirty awards from scientific organizations. One very special occasion was Kwolek's being inducted into the National Inventors Hall of Fame in Akron, Ohio, in 1995. The Hall of Fame honors such great creators as Thomas Edison

Kwolek was a pioneer for women scientists and received more than thirty awards for her work.

and the Wright brothers. Kwolek says she is tremendously honored to have her work exhibited in the same building as those inventors.

She is also very proud to have been a pioneer for women research scientists. "When I started, women were being urged to study to be teachers or nurses," she recalls. "Science was a man's field. But I never thought of myself as a woman scientist. I was just a scientist. I felt that if I studied hard, I would be as good as anyone else."[30]

She laughs about something she heard after her invention of Kevlar. It reminds her of how people took it for granted that all scientists were male. "People just assumed [Kevlar] had been invented by a man," she says. "A chemist in another company said, 'That guy who did the work . . . had to be a very outstanding chemist.' He referred to me as a guy." Kwolek says that at the time, Stephanie was not a popular name, as it is today. "He must have thought Stephanie was a man's name,"[31] she says.

"I Feel Very Lucky"

The thing that gives her the most pleasure, Kwolek says, is knowing that Kevlar has saved the lives of more than 3,000 police officers and hundreds of American soldiers fighting in Iraq and Afghanistan.

It has been a thrill for her to meet some of those people who were saved by the fiber she invented. "Years ago, I had a man who worked for the FBI who lived across the street from me. He was a very, very nice man. Every so often, he would bring someone over to meet me—police officers whose lives had been saved because they had worn a Kevlar vest. That was such a marvelous feeling."[32]

These U.S. Marines in Iraq are wearing Kevlar vests. It is the knowledge that Kevlar has saved so many lives that has given Kwolek the most pleasure in her life.

One police officer from Virginia even asked her to autograph his bulletproof vest, which had saved his life. So many researchers work their whole lives and do not make a discovery that can save lives, and that makes her feel very fortunate. "I feel very lucky,"[33] she says.

"An Exciting Time to Be Alive"

On July 31, 2007, Kwolek celebrated her eighty-fourth birthday. She remains very interested in science. "I look forward to each new journal coming out," she says. "I enjoy reading about new things that are happening."[34]

She likes going to schools to talk to young students about science and discovering things. "I take in some fibers, samples of Kevlar, so the children can feel them, see how they can't be destroyed. They seem to really be interested in that."[35]

Most of all, Kwolek hopes her work will inspire young people to think of science as a career. "I can't think of a better occupation," she says. "There are so many problems to be solved—taking better care of the environment, curing diseases. There are so many opportunities for discovery. It's really an exciting time to be alive."[36]

NOTES

Introduction: "Not in a Million Years"

1. Quoted in "IACP DuPont Kevlar Survivors' Club, interview with Corey G. Grogan. www2.dupont.com/Kevlar/en_US/ uses_apps/law_enforcement/survivors_club.html.
2. Telephone interview, Stephanie Kwolek, May 23, 2007.
3. Kwolek, May 23, 2007.

Chapter 1: A Childhood in Pennsylvania

4. Kwolek, May 23, 2007.
5. Kwolek, May 23, 2007.
6. Kwolek, May 23, 2007.
7. Kwolek, May 23, 2007.
8. Kwolek, May 23, 2007.
9. Kwolek, May 23, 2007.
10. Kwolek, May 23, 2007
11. Kwolek, May 23, 2007.
12. Kwolek, May 23, 2007.

Chapter 2: Choosing Research

13. Kwolek, May 23, 2007.
14. Kwolek, May 23, 2007.
15. Kwolek, May 23, 2007.
16. Kwolek, May 23, 2007.
17. Kwolek, May 23, 2007.

Chapter 3: "I Thought It Could Be a Mistake Somehow"

18. Quoted in "Insight: Stephanie Kwolek," http://web.mit.edu/

invent/www/ima/kwolek_intro.html.

19. Quoted in "Kevlar Inventor," http://invention.smithsonian. org/centerpieces/iap/inventorskwo4.html.

20. Quoted in "Insight: Stephanie Kwolek."

21. Quoted in Caitlyn Howell, "Stephanie Kwolek and Kevlar, the Wonder Fiber," Innovative Lives, http://invention.smith sonian.org/centerpieces/liveslecture05lhtml.

22. Quoted in "Insight: Stephanie Kwolek."

23. Kwolek, May 23, 2007.

24. Kwolek, May 23, 2007.

25. Kwolek, May 23, 2007.

Chapter 4: Kevlar and Beyond

26. Kwolek, May 23, 2007.

27. Kwolek, May 23, 2007.

28. Kwolek, May 23, 2007.

29. Quoted in Jon Swartz and Edward Iwata, "Invented to Save Gas, Kevlar Now Saves Lives," *USA Today,* April 16, 2003, p. B1.

30. Kwolek, May 23, 2007.

31. Quoted in Howell, "Stephanie Kwolek and Kevlar, the Wonder Fiber."

32. Kwolek, May 23, 2007.

33. Kwolek, May 23, 2007.

34. Kwolek, May 23, 2007.

35. Kwolek, May 23, 2007.

36. Kwolek, May 23, 2007.

GLOSSARY

bittersweet: A feeling that is a combination of happiness and sadness.

chemistry: A branch of science dealing with the basic makeup of different substances, especially molecules and atoms.

fiber: A single thread that can be woven into a fabric.

hypodermic needle: A fine needle used to insert medicine under the skin.

molecules: Made up of one or more atoms, it is the tiniest physical unit of a substance.

nylon: A type of human-made fiber used in clothing, rope, and other products.

perfectionist: Someone who tries to do everything correctly and well.

polymer: A chain of molecules arranged in a distinct pattern and shape.

puncture: To cause a hole in something.

solvent: A substance used to dissolve some other substance.

spinneret: A machine used to make polymer solutions into solid fibers.

synthetic: Human-made, rather than natural.

FOR FURTHER EXPLORATION

Books

Madeline P. Goodstein, *Plastics and Polymers Science Fair Projects: Using Hair Gel, Soda Bottles, and Slimy Stuff*. Berkeley Heights, NJ: Enslow, 2004. Very readable, with good explanations of the variety and makeup of polymers.

Ann Newmark, *Chemistry*. New York: Dorling Kindersley, 2000. Excellent illustrations showing the basics of chemistry and how researchers work.

Andrew Solway, *A History of Super Science*. Chicago: Raintree, 2006. A valuable first book about molecules and atoms—the basis of all chemistry.

Articles

"Women of the Hall: Stephanie Kwolek/National Women's Hall of Fame." www.greatwomen.org/women.php?action=view one&id=201.

Web Sites

The IACP/DuPont Kevlar Survivors' Club, DuPont. (www2. dupont.com/Kevlar/en_US/uses_apps/law_enforcement/survivo rs_club.html). An excellent site devoted to photographs, explanations, and details of the uses of Kevlar as well as interviews with people whose lives have been saved by Kevlar vests.

Kevlar—The Wonder Material, Lawrence Berkeley National Lab. (www.lbl.gov/MicroWorlds/Kevlar/). This site deals with the polymers that make up Kevlar. The explanations use diagrams and illustrations to make them understandable.

Polymer Basics, University of Southern Mississippi Department of Polymer Science. (www.pslc.ws/macrog/kidsmac/wiap.htm). Using cartoon characters and nontechnical jargon, this site explains polymers and their importance.

INDEX

B
Bulletproof vests, 6, 33–36

C
Carnegie Mellon University, 16, 17

D
DuPont, 19
  polymer research at, 21–22

G
Grogan, Corey, 6

K
Kevlar
  discovery of, 26–30
  early uses of, 33
  naming of, 31, 33
  strength of, 7
  use in bulletproof vests, 33–35
Kwolek, John (father), 9, 11–12

Kwolek, Nellie (mother), 9, 11, 12
Kwolek, Stephanie
  birth of, 9
  college years of, 16, 17
  discovers Kevlar polymer, 26–30
  on discovery of Kevlar, 7–8, 36
  at DuPont, 20–21, 22, 23, 24
  early goals of, 13, 15, 19
  on her parents, 11–12
  honors awarded to, 35
  on naming of Kevlar, 31, 33
  as pioneer for women, 36

M
Margaret Morrison Carnegie College, 16

N
National Inventors Hall of Fame (Akron, OH), 35–36

Nelson, David, 34–35
Nylon, 20

P
Polymers, 21
  creation of, 24–26

R
Research scientists, 24

Kwolek as pioneer for
  women as, 36

S
Spinnerets, 24–25
Synthetic fabrics, 19–20

W
World War II, 18

PICTURE CREDITS

ABOUT THE AUTHOR

Gail B. Stewart is the author of more than 200 books for children and young adults. The parent of three sons, she and her husband live in Minneapolis, Minnesota.